This
Unexpected
Jewel

This Unexpected Jewel

Reading the Diamond Sutra

Ken McLeod

UNFETTERED MIND MEDIA
WINDSOR, CALIFORNIA
USA

THIS UNEXPECTED JEWEL: READING THE DIAMOND SUTRA

The Mahayana Sutra called The Noble Perfection of Wisdom: The Vajra Cutter was translated from the Tibetan by Ken McLeod. The translation is from the edition in the Tibetan Kanjur: *The Vajra Cutter Sutra*, Tog Palace Manuscript, Tibetan Kanjur, vol. 51, Leh.

First edition, 2025

Published by Unfettered Mind Media, Windsor, California, United States of America

ISBN: 979-8-9861711-7-3
EPUB ISBN: 979-8-9861711-9-7

Library of Congress Control Number (LCCN): 2025917706

Printed in the United States of America

Cover photo: Ann Wheatley
Design by Happenstance Type-O-Rama

This book is a translation of a public domain Buddhist scripture. Any errors in translation are the responsibility of the translator.

For Agnes

Origin unknown,
This unexpected jewel
Lights these autumn days.

Contents

Introduction

WHEN I FIRST READ CHAPTER 3 in Red Pine's translation of the *Diamond Sutra*, my mind stopped:

> *However many beings there are . . . I shall liberate them all. And though I thus liberate countless beings, not a single being is liberated.*

I did not move or say anything for several minutes. There was only clarity, with no thought or movement of any kind. Later, it was clear that those sentences had revealed to me something about compassion and what it means to live awake. The experience changed me deeply, though I could not say what had been revealed or what had changed. I also understood what makes the *Diamond Sutra* special. The meaning of the sutra does not lie in understanding the words. Its meaning lies in what happens in you and to you when you hear or read it.

My aim in this book is to present the *Diamond Sutra* in English in such a way that the sutra evokes its clarity and power directly in you, the reader. This book is not an academic or scholastic work. It is a practitioner's translation, a translation made by a practitioner for other practitioners. It is for those who have taken the bodhisattva path as the basis of their life, or to put it another way, it is for those who seek to live in the world they actually live in rather than the world they think they live in.

What is a sutra? A sutra is a record of a meeting in which the student's mind and the teacher's mind come together. For such a meeting to come about, both teacher and student must drop their respective worlds and meet in an open space that neither of them defines. Only in that mystery does true communication and true learning take place. A sutra is a record of what happens in that space.

While the sutra is known in the English-speaking world as the *Diamond Sutra*, its full name in Sanskrit and Tibetan is *The Mahayana Sutra called The Noble Perfection of Wisdom — The Vajra Cutter*. The name *Diamond Sutra* is due to an accident, the kind of accident that often happens in translation from one culture to another.

When the 19th century German philologist Max Müller translated this sutra, out of deference to European readers he chose to use the word *diamond* for the Sanskrit word *vajra*. At that time, few Europeans had even heard the word *vajra*. His choice was understandable. A diamond was the hardest known substance, and like a vajra, a diamond could cut any substance without being cut itself. Müller's choice was adopted by subsequent scholars, and it became the accepted name in English.

For a variety of reasons, I have come to the conclusion that the *Diamond Sutra* was probably composed around the last century BCE or the first century CE. If so, it is one of the earliest Mahayana texts we have and among the earliest of the Perfection of Wisdom (*Prajñāpāramitā*) sutras. Although most people say that the sutra is about emptiness, the word *emptiness* does not even appear in the sutra. Nor does the sutra employ the Mahayana frameworks and vocabulary that developed later. In other words, in this sutra we see the Mahayana beginning to take shape.

The *Diamond Sutra* is the first book known to have been printed: a Chinese edition printed from xylographs in 868 CE. Printing made it possible for the sutra to spread widely throughout China. It became not only one of the principal texts in Chinese Buddhism but also the backbone of the Chan tradition and later the Zen tradition in Japan, Korea, and Vietnam. It may well have given rise to the centuries-long debate about sudden enlightenment and gradual enlightenment.

In the Tibetan tradition, the *Diamond Sutra* inspired the development of Chö (a.k.a. Chod). As a young nun, the 11th century mystic Machik Lapdrön read the Perfection of Wisdom sutras again and again. She became a devotee and an expert in this literature, to the point that her mastery was admired and acknowledged by contemporary Indian masters. In her teaching she combined shamanic, Mahayana, and Vajrayana elements to create a uniquely Tibetan form of mahamudra practice that she called Chö (Tib. gcod), or Cutting, taking the name from the formal name of the *Diamond Sutra — The Vajra Cutter*. In Chö the outer cutting of offering one's body to gods and demons cuts through hope and fear, the inner cutting of taking and sending (tonglen) cuts through self-cherishing, and the secret cutting of ineffable clarity (mahamudra) cuts through reactivity and confusion.

For centuries teachers have insisted that any conceptual understanding of the sutra is certain to be misleading. The *Diamond Sutra* is not a philosophical text. It does not present any ontology or metaphysics, and very little epistemology or ethics. Nor does it engage in debate with other philosophical schools. Its focus is direct and experiential. As its formal name implies, it cuts through any tendency to rely on conceptual understanding. By interrupting and confounding the conceptual mind, the sutra opens the reader to the possibility of experiencing the ineffable, clear knowing at the heart of all Buddhist practice.

Aside from guidance on setting a clear intention and a few other points, the sutra offers little in the way of explicit practice instruction. The sutra nevertheless encourages the cultivation of faith, generosity, and compassion. It carries a devotional undercurrent as it points us to a different way of experiencing life.

The wording in the sutra is simple, clear, and direct. The simplicity and clarity of the language belie the depth of the sutra. When we read the *Diamond Sutra*, especially when we read it aloud, certain passages stop conceptual thinking. Read regularly, the sutra disrupts our ordinary patterns of thought and reaction. In doing so, it makes possible a glimpse of the ineffable clarity to which it repeatedly points.

Reading the Sutra Aloud

MY HOPE FOR THIS SLIM VOLUME is that it inspires you, the reader, to take up the practice of sutra reading — in this case, reading the sutra aloud while standing. This practice engages your whole being, body, speech, and mind. Sutra reading goes back hundreds, if not thousands, of years, but it has fallen out of fashion, especially here in the West. That is regrettable, because to stand and read a sutra or any other text aloud is one of the best ways to form a relationship with that text that does not depend on conceptual understanding and to create the conditions in which you absorb directly what that text has to offer.

As in formal meditation practice, choose a well-lit place where you are free from disturbances during your reading session and the sound of your voice does not disturb others. For the *Diamond Sutra*, it is best to read the whole sutra in one reading — about 40 minutes in all. If that is not possible for you, then read a portion of it every day. When you have completed the sutra, then start from the beginning again.

BODY

Stand with your feet about shoulder-width apart, your weight evenly distributed with a little more than half your weight on the balls of your feet. Let your body straighten, as if you are being pulled up slightly by a thread connected to the very crown of your head. When you do that, your body straightens naturally, your head is level, your chin comes in slightly, and your spine and pelvis support your whole body. During the reading session, you may find it helpful to change the way you are holding the book or to shift your weight a little from one foot to another, but for the most part, keep your weight evenly distributed and your body straight but relaxed. Initially you may feel some discomfort, but after a few days, your body adjusts to standing, your legs and other muscles become stronger, and the small secondary muscles that keep you in balance naturally come into play.

If, for whatever reason, you are unable to stand, then read it in a sitting position. This is not an endurance practice. The aim is to build a relationship with the sutra in body, speech, and mind. Strain in the body is neither necessary nor helpful.

Position the sutra in front of you in a way that makes it easy to read. This edition of the sutra is probably light enough to hold in your hands. With other editions or other sutras, you may prefer to use a music stand to hold the text.

SPEECH

Stand quietly for a few minutes to let body, breath, and mind settle. When you are ready, start reading the sutra aloud. Read it in a natural voice, as if you were speaking to someone standing in front of you. Read it at a natural pace, not so quickly that you slur words or elide syllables, not so slowly that reading feels forced or contrived. As you read, listen to the sound of your own voice as if you were listening to someone else reading. When you do this, you naturally hear whether you are reading it too quickly or too slowly, whether there is any tension or strain in your voice, or whether you are reading in your own voice or someone else's.

MIND

As you read the sutra, let your mind rest. At first, let your mind rest on the sound of your voice as you read the sutra. Thoughts may come and go. If you are distracted and lose your place, take a breath, feel your feet on the ground and the presence of your whole body, and start again at the point you last remember reading. If at any point you find yourself thinking about the meaning of the sutra, regard that as you would any other thought and bring your attention back to the sound of your voice.

When you can read with relatively few distractions, then rest attention not only on the sound of your voice but also in your body. When you do so, you may find that your body naturally makes small adjustments in your posture. Usually the result is that your body feels more in balance and standing is easier and requires less energy. Again, if you find yourself thinking about the meaning of the sutra (or anything else, for that matter), come back to the sound of your voice and the presence of your body and continue reading.

READING WITHOUT THINKING

While you are doing all this, your body and mind are actually taking in the words and meaning of the sutra, even though you are not making any explicit effort to understand it. When read this way, the words of the sutra bypass the conceptual mind and engage body, speech, and mind directly. It often takes a while to become used to this way of reading because most of us are used to thinking about and arriving at a conceptual understanding of what we read. The purpose of this practice is quite different. It is to let the sutra speak directly to you. For that, you must listen, and to listen, you must learn how to be quiet inside as you engage the sutra.

At some point you may notice little shifts taking place as you read certain passages. Include the sensations of those shifts in your attention and rest there as you read. Some of those shifts may be emotional reactions that seem to come out of nowhere and take you right out of what you are doing. As before, as soon as you notice you have been distracted, take a breath, reconnect with your body, and return to the reading again. Other shifts include moments of clarity or understanding, the warmth of faith or devotion, heartfelt compassion or gratitude, or the cessation of conceptual thinking of any kind. When such positive shifts arise, you may try to hold onto them, extend them, or replicate them. The shifts themselves are in no way a problem, but as soon as you try to do anything with them, you have fallen into distraction. Again, when you notice that, take a breath, reconnect with your body, and return to reading.

As you learn to rest in these shifts, you may discover an ineffable clarity that is nothing other than your own mind shorn of confusion and reactivity. It may arise while you are reading, while you are meditating, or while you are going about your day. That clarity is what the *Diamond Sutra* teaches. In doing so, it opens the possibility of experiencing life in a completely different way.

Notes on Translation

THIS TRANSLATION IS BASED ON four principles: readability, clarity, integrity, and tone.

To ensure readability, I abide by the adage *"If it reads or sounds like a translation, it is not a translation."* Not all translators accept this adage for various reasons. More than a few people feel that English cannot and never will convey the depth of Buddhist teachings, and translations must employ foreign words.

My approach here is different. English can and does convey the depth of Buddhist teachings. It can do so without reliance on imported words or grammar. It does so best when the translation makes use of the richness of English vocabulary as well as the rhythm and cadence of English itself. For me, the above adage has proven to be a reliable measure of the quality of my own work as a translator. If I cannot express a phrase or a sentence in simple, clear English, one of two possibilities is indicated: either I do not understand the phrase experientially or I have not fully assimilated that understanding.

This sutra is a conversation between two people. I seek to convey the feeling of that conversation by paying attention to the natural cadences and rhythms of modern English. For vocabulary, the translation draws from the Teutonic and Old English roots and avoids academic, philosophical, or technical vocabularies as much as possible. Whether any piece of writing is in true English is immediately evident when it is read aloud. Because my intention is for this translation to be read aloud, it has to read well in English.

Clarity is equally important. My aim here is for the meaning to go into you before you even have a chance to think about it. This quality is especially important given that the sutra cuts through any and every tendency to intellectualize or conceptualize what it is pointing to. This clarity is achieved through careful word choice, simplicity of language and grammar, and precision and accuracy in rendering the meaning.

At the same time, I seek to uphold the integrity of the sutra by letting the sutra stand on its own two feet. By and large, the sutra does not use much technical vocabulary. Nor does it rely on Buddhist terminology and perspectives that developed centuries later. It uses a variety of methods to point the reader to what cannot be put in words: comparisons that confound the mind; analogies and metaphors that stretch the imagination; repetition, repetition, and more repetition; and seeming paradoxes and contradictions that mysteriously cease to be paradoxes and contradictions when their meaning sinks in. All these methods are intended to elicit shifts in how you know and how you experience your mind and your life. For this reason, I have eschewed as much as possible the ontological and essentialist language of Western thought in favor of grammar and word choice that elicit shifts in direct experience.

One of the biggest challenges has been to find a tone in English that conveys the sense of reverence, respect, and wonder that permeates the sutra. English no longer has a sacred or high formal mode of speech. That died out toward the end of the 19th century. I have made no effort to resuscitate it or to imitate archaic or elevated styles of speech or writing. Instead, I have sought to let a sense of the sacred emerge through the intimacy of the conversation, the natural cadence of the English language, and the immediacy of the meaning. In this way a sense of reverence, awe, and wonder emerges through language that is respectful, clear, precise, and accurate.

A few translation choices call for explicit mention because they differ from most other translations.

Dharma (Tib. chos) Various sources attribute eight, ten, or up to eighteen different meanings to this word. Among the most common are "truth," "law," "duty," "teaching," "a way of doing something," "instruction on how to do something," "religion," "spiritual activity," "transmission," and the meaning most prevalent in this sutra, "an irreducible element of how we experience life." Even so, in several sentences in the sutra, one could substitute any of four or five of the above meanings, and the sentence would still make perfect sense. In order to preserve this play on words, Paul Harrison, Red Pine, and several other translators chose not to translate the word *dharma* at all.

When I started to teach, I noticed how the use of the word *dharma* for an element of experience has the same effect on most readers as the word *phenomenon*: it plunges them straight into the Cartesian dualism on which Kant based his thinking. For this reason, I have long used the word *experience* to translate *dharma* when it refers to an irreducible element of experience. Unlike *dharma* or *phenomenon*, the word *experience* often elicits awe and wonder at the miracle of experience itself. In short, I have seen too many eyes light up when I use the word *experience* in this context. A typical comment from a student is "Oh, this is not about things out there, but how I experience life."

Goodness (Skt. punya, Tib. bsod nams) The transactional and quantitative connotations of merit have always put me off, particularly in the phrase "the accumulation of merit." For this reason, I long ago chose to translate *punya* as "goodness." Then "the accumulation of merit" becomes "the generation of goodness," a translation that emphasizes the ethical and relational qualities of virtuous action without implying a transactional or quantitative framework. In Asian culture this term is often used the way Western culture uses the word *luck* (good things happen to good people) with the unfortunate added implication that virtue can be used to purchase good luck.

Arhat (Tib. dgra bcom pa) An arhat is a person of great virtue who is worthy of reverence or worthy of offerings. The Tibetan has a very different meaning. Formed probably from a folk etymology, it means "one who has conquered the enemy," the enemy being emotional reactions. Following the Sanskrit, I have chosen the word *saint* to reflect the original connotation of "one who is worthy."

A veritable constellation of terms refers to Buddha in this and many other sutras. The Sanskrit words for the terms in this constellation are *Buddha, Bhagavan, Tathagata, Sugata,* and *Tathagata Arhat Samyaksambuddha.*

Buddha is the term that refers to a person who has woken up. When this sutra was written, *buddha* was a not uncommon term of respect for revered teachers of any religious tradition. I chose not to translate the word *Buddha* when it refers to a person because the word has now become a word with this meaning in English.

However, *buddha* can also be a verb in both Sanskrit and Tibetan. As a verb, *buddha* means "to be awake" or "to have awakened," and that is how I translate it in those instances.

Bhagavan (Tib. bcom ldan 'das) was also a common mode of address in ancient India for individuals venerated for their religious understanding. It is how Subhuti addresses the Buddha throughout the sutra. The Tibetan translation of *bhagavan* is based on a folk etymology that packs a lot of meaning into each syllable: *bcom* (pron. "chom") represents arhat or saint, *ldan* (pron. "den") represents having all good qualities, and *'das* (pron. "dé") represents nirvana. In other words, it is coded language to which no translation can do justice. The most common translation from the Sanskrit is "lord." However, in English, *lord* has unavoidable feudal and military connotations. Because the principal connotation of *bhagavan* is "one worthy of veneration," I have chosen the phrase "Most Honored."

Tathagata (Tib. de bzhin gshegs pa) is a bit of a mystery. The most common translation is based on the etymology of the word: "one who has gone thus," giving rise to "Thus Gone" or "Thus Gone One." However, Richard Gombrich notes that as a suffix, *-gata* can also mean "is" or "being" — "one who is thus."

In this sutra, the word *tathagata* is used by both Buddha and Subhuti to refer to Buddha, particularly when something Buddha has previously taught is being quoted. In other words, Buddha refers to himself in the third person. On these occasions, it seems that both Buddha and Subhuti are regarding what Buddha said on the topic in question as coming not from a conventional conceptual mind but from thusness itself. This observation led me to consider translating *tathagata* as "thusness."

The play on words between *tathagata* as a person and *tathagata* as thusness runs throughout the sutra. For instance, in Chapter 2:

> *Thusness guides bodhisattva-mahasattvas with supreme guidance. Thusness entrusts bodhisattva-mahasattvas with supreme trust.*

To retain that play on words, I have chosen to translate *tathagata* as "Thusness," capitalizing the latter because it often does refer to a person. This is a controversial choice, but it works well in most instances. In the places where it is a bit of a stretch, I ask the reader's indulgence.

Sugata (Tib. bde bar gshegs pa) was also a common term of respect that originally referred to someone who takes deep joy in life. For this reason, I have translated it as "Most Joyous," even though it is usually rendered as "one who has gone or come to bliss."

Tathagata Arhat Samyaksambuddha is the formal title for full buddhas. Many translators have chosen to dispense with this compound title and use a single word or shorter phrase instead — "Realized One," for example. The title occurs throughout the sutra. To retain the respect and reverence inherent in this title, I have retained the compound form and rendered it as "Full and Complete Buddha, Thusness, and Saint," with the words in the order that English usually uses for compound titles. When it refers to a specific person, it is capitalized. When it refers to that level of attainment, it is not capitalized.

Non-self (Skt. anatman, Tib. bdag med) is central to all Buddhist teachings. Several years ago, I happened upon a note by Paul Harrison in which he distinguishes between two interpretations of non-self. With his permission, here is what he writes:

> When a word (X) is negated by the a- or an- prefix, one can translate it either as a karmadhåraya (not X, no X, non-X) or as a bahuvrīhi (X-less, lacking X, having no X). Thus to say of someone that he is aputra could mean that he is not a son or no son (with the possible implication that he is in fact a son

but one not worthy of the name), or that he is son-less, i.e. he has no sons.

and

It is interesting that only the Tibetan translation opts here, as it does throughout the text, for the bahuvrīhi *interpretation (X med pa or X ma mchis pa).*

When applied to the word *self, non-self* can be interpreted on the one hand as absolute negation — as "no self" or "a self does not exist" — or, on the other hand, as lacking or being without self — selfless or without a sense of self. The majority of Chinese translations of the *Diamond Sutra* have followed Kumarajiva's interpretation of absolute negation, and most Western translations of this sutra have followed suit. In Tibetan, however, the other interpretation, that of lacking or being without, is clearly indicated by the grammar, and it is this interpretation that I follow in the translation presented here.

Much more could be written about the ways I chose to translate this sutra. The more I read and digest the sutra, the deeper my respect and appreciation for it. A detailed commentary is in the works. It first explores the principal themes in the sutra and how they weave together. Then it offers an annotated version of the translation with comments on both the meaning of the sutra and the translation choices made to convey the meaning. Here are three instances that are directly relevant to the reading of the sutra aloud.

Verbal punctuation Both Sanskrit and Tibetan lack punctuation marks and make use of verbal punctuation to indicate who is speaking to whom — "Buddha said to Subhuti" or "Subhuti replied to Buddha." I have omitted this verbal punctuation and made use of English punctuation (quotation marks, commas, and paragraphing) to indicate, without loss of clarity, who is speaking to whom. The result is an English text that reads more like an actual conversation.

Chapter titles In both the Sanskrit and Tibetan versions of the sutra, the sutra is not divided into chapters. As Red Pine and others have noted, the chapter divisions were introduced into the Chinese tradition by Prince Chao-ming in the 6th century in an attempt to clarify the meaning of the sutra. This prince was the eldest son of Emperor Wu, the same emperor who imprisoned Bodhidharma when Bodhidharma first visited him.

Prince Chao-ming's chapter divisions leave a lot to be desired. The chapters range in length from a single paragraph to several pages, and they do little to clarify the sutra in the longer chapters. The titles he gave the chapters often introduce ideas and understandings that were not present when the sutra itself was composed. I have left out the titles but retained the divisions for two reasons. They make references to different parts of the sutra easier to find, and they facilitate the comparison of different translations.

Rhythm Wherever possible, I have used the rhythms of English to bring out how to read the sutra. For instance, in most translations, the opening sentence usually follows the Chinese "Thus have I heard." In the translation offered here, the opening sentence is "Here is what I once heard said." The three long beats — once, heard, and said — are intended to nudge readers to read with attention — not only to what they are reading, but also to what they experience while they are reading.

The Mahayana Sutra called The Noble Perfection of Wisdom

The Vajra Cutter

I BOW TO ALL BUDDHAS AND BODHISATTVAS.

§1

This is what I once heard said. The Most Honored was residing near Shravasti in Jeta's Grove at the Provider for the Defenseless Park along with a large gathering of twelve hundred and fifty monks and a great many bodhisattva-mahasattvas.

That morning the Most Honored put on his robes, picked up his alms bowl, and went to the city of Shravasti to seek alms. When he returned from his alms round in Shravasti, he made offerings with the alms food, ate what remained, put away his robes and bowl, and washed his feet. He sat down on the seat prepared for him, crossed his legs, straightened his body, and rested in clear presence.

Then many monks gathered around him. They bowed, touched their heads to his feet, walked around him three times, and sat down together.

§2

On this occasion Venerable Subhuti was among those who had gathered. Subhuti rose from his seat and bared his right shoulder. He knelt with his right knee on the ground, joined his palms together, and bowed to the Most Honored. Then with these words he presented his question. "It is truly inspiring, Most Honored, truly inspiring, Most Joyous, the extent to which bodhisattva-mahasattvas are guided with supreme guidance by a full and complete buddha, thusness, and saint and the extent to which bodhisattva-mahasattvas are entrusted with supreme trust by a full and complete buddha, thusness, and saint.

"Most Honored, how should those who have entered the way of the bodhisattva live, how should they practice, and how should they hold their minds?"

The Most Honored responded to Venerable Subhuti with these words, "Well said, well said, Subhuti. That is how it is, Subhuti. That is how it is. Thusness guides bodhisattva-mahasattvas with supreme guidance. Thusness entrusts bodhisattva-mahasattvas with supreme trust. Therefore, Subhuti, listen carefully and take these words to heart as I tell you how those who have entered the way of the bodhisattva should live, how they should practice, and how they should hold their minds."

"Please do so, Most Honored," he replied. Venerable Subhuti then readied himself to listen to the Most Honored.

§3

The Most Honored said to Subhuti, "To your question, one who has entered the way of the bodhisattva should set their intention by thinking: 'However many sentient beings are counted as sentient beings, whether they are born from eggs, born from wombs, born from heat and moisture, or born miraculously, whether they have bodies or do not have bodies, whether they conceptualize, do not conceptualize, or neither conceptualize nor do not conceptualize — however many sentient beings in the realm of sentient beings are counted as sentient beings — I shall bring them all the way to nirvana, to the vastness of the nirvana in which no aggregate remains. Further, although sentient beings beyond measure come all the way to nirvana, no sentient being comes all the way to nirvana.'

"Why do I say that? Because, Subhuti, if a bodhisattva engages the concept of sentient being, they should not be called a bodhisattva. Why do I say that? Subhuti, anyone who engages the concept of sentient being, the concept of living being, or the concept of individual being should not be called a bodhisattva.

§4

"Further, Subhuti, bodhisattvas give what they give without dwelling on substance. They give what they give without dwelling on anything. They give what they give without dwelling on form. They give what they give without dwelling on sound, smell, taste, touch, or thought. Subhuti, bodhisattvas give what they give without dwelling on even the thought of a defining characteristic. Why do I say that? Subhuti, when bodhisattvas give what they give without dwelling on anything, the amount of goodness, Subhuti, is not easy to measure.

"Subhuti, what do you think? Is the space to the east easy to measure?"

"Indeed no, Most Honored."

"In the same way, is the space to the south, to the west, to the north, above, below, to the intermediate directions, indeed, to any of the ten directions easy to measure?"

"Indeed no, Most Honored."

"Subhuti, in the same way, when bodhisattvas give what they give without dwelling on anything the amount of goodness is not easy to measure.

§5

"Subhuti, what do you think? Do you look at Thusness as showing the physical signs of excellence?"

"Indeed no, Most Honored. I do not look at Thusness as showing the physical signs of excellence. Why do I say that? Because Thusness teaches that that which shows the physical signs of excellence does not have the physical signs of excellence."

"Subhuti, that which shows the physical signs of excellence is misleading. That which does not show the physical signs of excellence is not misleading. Therefore, look at Thusness as having and not having the physical signs."

§6

"Most Honored, in the future, in the final five hundred years when the Holy Teachings have completely disintegrated, will there be any sentient beings who develop a correct understanding of the explanation of sutras such as this?"

"Subhuti, do not ask, 'In the future, in the final five hundred years when the Holy Teachings have completely disintegrated, will there be any sentient beings who develop a correct understanding of the explanation of sutras such as this?'

"In the future, in the final five hundred years when the Holy Teachings have completely disintegrated, bodhisattva-mahasattvas will arise who are ethical, capable, and intelligent. Moreover, Subhuti, these bodhisattva-mahasattvas will not be those who have attended one buddha. They will not be those who have generated virtue under one buddha. Subhuti, bodhi-sattva-mahasattvas will arise who have attended many hundreds if not thousands of buddhas and have generated virtue under many hundreds if not thousands of buddhas.

"Anyone who, if only for a moment, develops faith in the explanation of sutras such as this one, Thusness knows them, Subhuti. Thusness sees them, Subhuti. Subhuti, all those sentient beings generate and amass incalculable amounts of goodness.

"Why do I say that? Because, Subhuti, these bodhi-sattva-mahasattvas do not engage a sense of self, nor the concept of sentient being, nor the concept of living being, nor the concept of individual being. Subhuti, these bodhisattva-mahasattvas do not engage the con-cept of experience or the concept of the absence of experience. They do not engage concepts or even the absence of concepts.

"Why do I say that? Because, Subhuti, if these bodhisattva-mahasattvas engage the concept of expe-rience, that would lead them to hold to a sense of self, a sentient being, a living being, or an individual being. Moreover, if they engage the concept of the absence of experience, that would also lead them to hold to a sense of self, a sentient being, a living being, or an individual being.

"Why do I say that? Again, Subhuti, because bodhisattvas should not incorrectly engage any experience, nor any absence of experience. With that in mind, if Thusness teaches that all those who know how the teachings are expressed as being like a raft should let go of experience, there is no need to mention the absence of experience.

§7

"What do you think, Subhuti? With respect to Thusness, is there any such experience as coming to full and complete buddhahood, to the supreme and utter completeness of awakening? Has Thusness revealed any such experience?"

"Most Honored, as I understand what the Most Honored has said, with respect to Thusness there is no such experience as coming to full and complete buddhahood, to the supreme and utter completeness of awakening. Thusness has not revealed any such experience. Why do I say that? Thusness does not engage or describe the utter and complete awakening or revealing of any such experience because such an experience is neither present nor absent. What is the point here? The point is that the unconditioned is what differentiates worthy persons."

§8

"Subhuti, what do you think? Suppose a son or daughter of good family makes a gift of this great thousand-world-system of a billion worlds filled to overflowing with the seven jewels. From this basis does the son or daughter of good family generate a great quantity of goodness?"

"Most Honored, great indeed. Most Joyous, great indeed. From this basis the son or daughter of good family does generate a great quantity of goodness. What is the point here? The point is, Most Honored, that very quantity of goodness is without quantity. Therefore, Thusness teaches it is a quantity of goodness."

"Subhuti, compared to any son or daughter of good family who makes a gift of this great thousand-world-system of a billion worlds filled to overflowing with the seven jewels, anyone who engages even one four-line verse from how these teachings are expressed, teaches it correctly, and explains it to others, from that basis, that person generates a much greater quantity of goodness, incalculably, immeasurably greater.

"Why do I say that? Because, Subhuti, from this comes the supreme and complete awakening that is full and complete buddhahood, thusness, and sainthood. All the most honored, the buddhas, are born from this. Why do I say that? Subhuti, because Thusness teaches that the so-called teachings of full awakening are without teachings of full awakening. Accordingly, they are called teachings of full awakening.

§9

"Subhuti, what do you think? Do stream-enterers think, 'I have attained the result stream-enterer'?"

"No, indeed, Most Honored. What is the point here? The point, Most Honored, is that they have not entered anything. Therefore they are called stream-enterers. They do not enter form, nor sound, nor smell, nor taste, nor touch, nor thought. Therefore they are called stream-enterers. Most Honored, if a stream-enterer were to think, 'I have attained the result stream-enterer,' right there, he or she engages a sense of self, engages being a sentient being, engages being a living being, and engages being an individual being."

"What do you think, Subhuti? Do once-returners think, 'I have attained the result once-returner'?"

"No, indeed, Most Honored. What is the point here? The point is that there is no such experience as being a once-returner. Therefore, they are called once-returners."

"What do you think, Subhuti? Do non-returners think, 'I have attained the result non-returner'?"

"No, indeed, Most Honored. What is the point here? The point is that there is no such experience as being a non-returner. Therefore, they are called non-returners."

"What do you think, Subhuti? Do saints think, 'I have attained the result sainthood'?"

"No, indeed, Most Honored. What is the point here? The point is that there is no such experience as sainthood. Most Honored, if a saint thinks, 'I have attained sainthood,' right there they engage a sense of self. They engage being a sentient being, engage being a living being, and engage being an individual being.

"Most Honored, Full and Complete Buddha, Thusness, and Saint has declared that I am the foremost of those who dwell free of emotional reactions and, Most Honored, that I am indeed a saint, free from the reactivity of attraction. Most Honored, I do not think, 'I am a saint.' Most Honored, if I were to think, 'I am a saint,' Thusness would not declare of me, 'Subhuti, son of good family, you are the foremost of those who dwell free of emotional reactions. Because you do not dwell on anything, you dwell free of emotional reactions.'"

§10

"Subhuti, what do you think? Did Thusness receive any transmission from Dipankara, Full and Complete Buddha, Thusness, and Saint?"

"No, indeed, Most Honored. Thusness did not receive any transmission from Dipankara, Full and Complete Buddha, Thusness, and Saint."

"Subhuti, if some bodhisattva says, 'I will create beautifully laid out fields of awareness,' what he says would not be true. Why do I say that? Because, Subhuti, Thusness teaches that what are called beautifully laid out fields of awareness are not beautifully laid out. Thus, they are called beautifully laid out fields of awareness.

"Subhuti, for this reason, bodhisattva-mahasattvas should give rise to intentions that are not set like this, intentions that are not set in any way, intentions that are not set in form, intentions that are not set in sound, or smell, or taste, or touch, or even thought.

"Subhuti, say, for example, a person were to have a body like this, say, like Mount Meru, the king of mountains. Subhuti, what do you think? Would that be a large body?"

"Indeed, Most Honored, that would be a large body. Indeed, Most Joyous, that would be a large body. What is the point here? The point is that Thusness teaches that it has no substance. Hence it is called a body. It is called a body because, as Thusness teaches, it has no substance."

§11

"Subhuti, what do you think? If every grain of sand in the Ganges valley was turned into a Ganges valley, would the amount of sand in those valleys be substantial?"

"The number of Ganges valleys would be substantial indeed, Most Honored, to say nothing of the grains of sand in them."

"Subhuti, listen carefully and take this in. If every one of those grains of sand were a world-system and a man or a woman were to fill all of them with the seven jewels and offer that as a gift to every full and complete buddha, thusness, and saint, Subhuti, what do you think? From that basis would that man or woman generate a lot of goodness?"

"A lot, indeed, Most Honored. A lot, indeed, Most Joyous. From that basis that man or woman would generate a lot of goodness."

"Subhuti, compared to someone who offers a gift of that many world-systems filled with the seven jewels to every full and complete buddha, thusness, and saint, a person who, having engaged just one four-line verse from how these teachings are expressed, explains it and also teaches it correctly to others generates from that basis far more goodness — incalculably, immeasurably more.

§12

"Further, Subhuti, wherever one person recites or teaches even only a four-line verse from how these teachings are expressed, gods, humans, and titans together make that place a shrine for the world. If that is the case, what is to be said about someone who takes up how these teachings are expressed, cherishes it, studies it, takes it to heart, attends to it appropriately, and comes to inspire awe and wonder in others? A buddha will even dwell in that place, and other masters will make their homes there as well."

§13

Then Subhuti asked the Most Honored, "Most Honored, what is the name of how these teachings are expressed? How does one engage it?"

"Subhuti, how these teachings are expressed is called The Perfection of Wisdom. Engage it accordingly. Why do I say that? Because, Subhuti, what Thusness teaches as the perfection of wisdom is itself without perfection. Therefore it is called The Perfection of Wisdom. Subhuti, what do you think? Has Thusness given any such teaching?"

"Most Honored, Thusness has not given any such teaching."

"What do you think, Subhuti? Are there many dust particles present in a great thousand-world-system of a billion worlds?"

"Yes, Most Honored, many dust particles indeed. Yes, Most Joyous, many dust particles indeed. What is the point here? The point is, Most Honored, that Thusness teaches that any such dust particle is without a particle. Therefore, it is called a dust particle. Any such world-system Thusness teaches that it is without a system. Therefore, it is called a world-system."

"What do you think, Subhuti? Do you look at a full and complete buddha, thusness, and saint by means of the thirty-two physical signs of a great person?"

"No, indeed, Most Honored. What is the point here? The point is that what Thusness teaches as the thirty-two signs of a great person Thusness teaches as being without sign. Therefore they are called the thirty-two signs of Thusness."

"Subhuti, if a man or woman were to give away their own body as many times as there are grains of sand in the Ganges valley, and if someone were to take just one four-line verse from how these teachings are expressed and teach it to others, on that basis the latter would generate incalculably, immeasurably more goodness."

§14

At this point, the depth of these teachings moved Subhuti to weep. After he had wiped away his tears, Subhuti said to the Most Honored, "How these teachings are expressed in the way that Thusness teaches is awe-inspiring, Most Honored. It is awe-inspiring, Most Joyous. Most Honored, since timeless awareness took birth in me, I have never heard these teachings expressed in this way. Most Honored, with this explanation of the sutra those sentient beings who give rise to a correct understanding will be truly remarkable. What is the point here? The point, Most Honored, is that that which is a correct understanding is without understanding. Therefore, Thusness calls it a correct understanding.

"Most Honored, as for reflection and trust in the explanation of how these teachings are expressed, for me to trust it is not particularly remarkable. However, Most Honored, in the end of times, at the end of this age, in the last five hundred years, those who take up how these teachings are expressed, cherish it, read it, and take it to heart will be truly remarkable.

"Further, Most Honored, they will not engage the concept of self, the concept of sentient being, the concept of living being, or the concept of individual being. What is the point here? The point here, Most Honored, is that the concept of self, the concept of sentient being, the concept of living being, the concept of individual being, and all such concepts are without concept. What is the point here? The point is that the most honoreds, the buddhas, are free of concepts."

"That is correct, Subhuti, that is correct. Those sentient beings who are not frightened or daunted or disheartened by this sutra are truly remarkable. Why do I say that? Because, Subhuti, Thusness teaches this perfection. What Thusness teaches as the greatest of the perfections, countless buddhas, the most honoreds, have taught, too. Therefore it is called the greatest of the perfections.

"Again, Subhuti, whatever is the perfection of patience of Thusness, it is without perfection. Why do I say that? Because, Subhuti, when King Kalingka cut off my limbs and my other extremities, no concept of any kind arose in me. No concept of self, no concept of sentient being, no concept of living being, and no concept of individual being arose. Nor did I become senseless. Why do I say that? Because, Subhuti, if on that occasion the concept of a person arose in me, the concept of hostility would also have arisen at the same time. If the concept of sentient being, the concept of living being, or the concept of individual being had arisen, the concept of hostility would have arisen at the same time.

"Subhuti, through my higher perception, I know that in the past, for a series of five hundred lives, I was a seer named Patient Speaker and the concept of self did not arise in me, nor did the concept of sentient being, living being, or individual being. In the same way, Subhuti, bodhisattva-mahasattvas cease to engage concepts and set their intention on ultimate, full, and complete awakening. They also set their intention without dwelling on form. They set their intention without dwelling on sound, smell, taste, touch, or thought. They set their intention without dwelling on the absence of thought. They set their intention without dwelling on anything. Why do I say that? Because any dwelling is without dwelling. In this way Thusness teaches, 'Bodhisattvas give what they give without dwelling.'

"Further, Subhuti, for the sake of all beings, a bodhisattva practices giving completely in this way. Any concept of a sentient being is itself without concept. All sentient beings of whom Thusness teaches are themselves without being. Why do I say that? Because, Subhuti, Thusness teaches what is correct, what is true, and how it is. Because Thusness teaches how it is, the teaching is without error. Further, Subhuti, in the experience which Thusness has utterly and completely awakened and taught, there is nothing true and there is nothing false.

"Subhuti, it is like this: regard a bodhisattva who has fallen into substantiality and practices giving completely as, for example, like a man with eyes who does not see anything in the dark. Subhuti, it is like this: regard a bodhisattva who has not fallen into substantiality and practices giving completely as, for example, like a man with eyes who, when the sun rises in the morning, sees the whole range of shapes and forms.

"Subhuti, Thusness knows and Thusness sees any son or daughter of good family who takes up how these teachings are expressed, cherishes it, reads it, takes it to heart, and teaches it correctly and widely to others. All these sentient beings generate immeasurable quantities of goodness.

§15

"Further, Subhuti, if one morning a man or woman were to give away their body as many times as there are grains of sand in the Ganges valley, and in the afternoon and in the evening, they were to give away their body as many times as there are grains of sand in the Ganges valley, and they were to give away their body counting in this manner for a hundred thousand million billion eons, and if someone were to hear how these teachings are expressed and not reject it, on that basis, the latter would generate far more goodness, incalculably, immeasurably more, to say nothing of someone who writes it out, takes it up, cherishes it, reads it, takes it to heart, and teaches it widely to others correctly and completely. Subhuti, how these teachings are expressed is incomparable and inconceivable, and its karmic ripening is also inconceivable.

"Thusness teaches that how these teachings are expressed is for those who are properly established in the supreme way and for those who are properly established at the highest level of the way. Thusness knows and Thusness sees anyone who takes up how these teachings are expressed, cherishes it, reads it, and takes it to heart, and teaches it correctly and widely to others. These sentient beings come to have immeasurable quantities of goodness. Having quantities of goodness that are inconceivable, incomparable, inestimable, and immeasurable, these sentient beings will carry part of my awakening on their shoulders.

"Why do I say that? Subhuti, all those drawn to lesser aims are unable to listen to how these teachings are expressed. Nor can it be heard, cherished, read, or taken to heart by those who hold to self, those who hold to sentient being, those who hold to living being, and those who hold to individual being, because it is not possible.

"Further, Subhuti, any place where this sutra is taught becomes a place worthy of offerings from the whole world with its gods, humans, and titans. It becomes a place worthy of bows and worthy of circumambulations — like a stupa.

§16

"Subhuti, those sons or daughters of a good family who take up sutras such as this one, cherish them, read them, and take them to heart will be troubled. They will be tormented. Why do I say that? Because, Subhuti, the unwholesome actions that these sentient beings did in earlier lives, the actions that would lead them to be born in the lower realms, will trouble them in this very life. They will be cleansed of the unwholesome actions of former lives and they will attain the awakening of buddha.

"Subhuti, through my higher perception, uncountably uncountable eons ago — long, long before Dipankara, Full and Complete Buddha, Thusness, and Saint — I served eighty-four hundred thousand million billion buddhas and served them faithfully. Subhuti, of the quantity of goodness from my serving these buddhas and serving them faithfully and the quantity of someone who, in the last five hundred years of the end of times, takes up this sutra, cherishes it, reads it, and takes it to heart, the former does not remotely approach a hundredth, a thousandth, or a hundred-thousandth of the latter. The latter does not permit any measure based on counting, division, tally, analogy, comparison, or genesis.

"Subhuti, if I were to describe what a great quantity of goodness sons or daughters of noble families would earn at that time, the sheer quantity of goodness of those sons or daughters of noble families, it would leave sentient beings confused and trembling. Subhuti, know that because how these teachings are expressed is inconceivable, its karmic ripening is also inconceivable."

§17

"Most Honored, how does one who has correctly entered the way of the bodhisattva live, how does one practice, how does one take hold of mind?"

"Subhuti, for this, one who has correctly entered the way of the bodhisattva sets this clear intention by thinking, 'I shall bring all sentient beings all the way to nirvana, to the vastness of the nirvana in which no aggregate remains. Further, although sentient beings beyond measure come all the way to nirvana, no sentient being comes all the way to nirvana.'

"Why do I say that? Because, Subhuti, if a bodhisattva engages the concept of sentient being, he or she should not be called a bodhisattva. Why do I say that? Subhuti, anyone who engages the concept of sentient being, the concept of living being, or the concept of individual being should not be called a bodhisattva. Why do I say that? Because, Subhuti, there is no experience called 'one who has correctly entered the way of the bodhisattva.'

"Subhuti, what do you think? Did Thusness have any such experience as supreme, pure, and complete awakening into full buddhahood comparable to Thusness Dipankara?"

"Most Honored, Thusness did not have any such experience as supreme, pure, and complete awakening into full buddhahood comparable to Thusness Dipankara."

"That is right, Subhuti, that is right. Thusness did not have any such experience as supreme, pure, and complete awakening into full buddhahood comparable to Thusness Dipankara.

"Subhuti, if Thusness had had some such experience of actual complete buddhahoood, Thusness Dipankara would not have predicted, 'Sometime in the future, young man, you will be called Shakyamuni, Full and Complete Buddha, Thusness, and Saint.' Subhuti, therefore, because Thusness did not have any such experience as supreme, full, and complete awakening into utterly complete buddhahood, Thusness Dipankara predicted, 'Young man, sometime in the future, you will be called Shakyamuni, Full and Complete Buddha, Thusness, and Saint.'

"Why do I say that? Subhuti, because the word 'thusness' is a synonym for 'truly thus.' Subhuti, if someone were to say, 'Full and Complete Buddha, Thusness, and Saint came to supreme full and complete awakening into utterly complete buddhahood,' that would be misleading. Why do I say that? Because, Subhuti, Thusness has no such experience as supreme full and complete awakening into utterly complete buddhahood. Subhuti, for Thusness, any experience in which one is utterly and completely awake is neither true nor false. Therefore, Thusness teaches that all experience is called buddha experience. Subhuti, what is called all experience, all of it is without experience. Thus, all experience is called buddha experience.

"Subhuti, here is how it is. As an example, it is like a man with a body, a really large body."

"Most Honored, when Thusness teaches about a man with a body, with a really large body, Thusness teaches that the body is bodyless. Therefore it is said that the man has a body, a really large body."

"Subhuti, that is right. Any bodhisattva who says, 'I bring all sentient beings all the way across to nirvana,' should not be called a bodhisattva. Why do I say that? Subhuti, is there any such experience as being a bodhisattva?"

"No, indeed, Most Honored."

"Therefore, Subhuti, Thusness teaches that in all experience, there are no sentient beings, no living beings, and no individual beings.

"Subhuti, if a bodhisattva says, 'I shall create beautifully laid out fields of awareness,' the same should be said of him or her. Why do I say that? Because, Subhuti, Thusness teaches that with regard to beautifully laid out fields of awareness, what are called beautifully laid out fields of awareness are not beautifully laid out. That is why they are called beautifully laid out fields of awareness.

"Subhuti, of any bodhisattva who understands 'all experience is without self,' Full and Complete Buddha, Thusness, and Saint says, 'That is a bodhisattva.'

§18

"Subhuti, what do you think? Does Thusness have physical sight?"

"Most Honored, yes, yes, indeed. Thusness has physical sight."

"Subhuti, what do you think? Does Thusness have divine sight?"

"Most Honored, yes, yes, indeed. Thusness has divine sight."

"Subhuti, what do you think? Does Thusness have wisdom sight?"

"Most Honored, yes, yes, indeed. Thusness has wisdom sight."

"Subhuti, what do you think? Does Thusness have spiritual sight?"

"Most Honored, yes, yes, indeed. Thusness has spiritual sight."

"Subhuti, what do you think? Does Thusness have awake sight?"

"Most Honored, yes, yes, indeed. Thusness has awake sight."

"Subhuti, what do you think? If all the grains of sand in the Ganges valley were to become Ganges valleys, and all the grains of sand in them were to become world-systems, would there be many world-systems?"

"Yes, yes, indeed, Most Honored. There would be many world-systems, indeed."

"Subhuti, I am fully aware of the mind-streams of as many sentient beings as there are in those world-systems. Why do I say that? Because, Subhuti, Thusness teaches that what is called a mind-stream is without stream. Therefore it is called a mind-stream. Why do I say that? Because, Subhuti, the past mind is not found, the future mind is not found, and the present mind is not found.

§19

"Subhuti, what do you think? Suppose a son or daughter of a noble family filled to overflowing this great thousand-world-system of a billion worlds with the seven jewels and gave it away. On this basis, would such a person generate much goodness?"

"Much indeed, Most Honored. Much indeed, Most Joyous."

"That is right, Subhuti. That is right. On this basis, a son or daughter of good family would generate a great quantity of goodness. Subhuti, if there were such a quantity of goodness, Thusness would not call it a quantity of goodness.

§20

"Subhuti, what do you think? Do you see Thusness as the fully formed physical body?"

"No, indeed, Most Honored. I do not see Thusness as the fully formed physical body. Why do I say that? Because, Most Honored, Thusness has taught that that which is called a fully formed physical body or a completely formed physical body is not fully formed. Therefore, it is called a fully formed physical body."

"What do you think, Subhuti? Do you see Thusness as the physical signs of excellence?"

"No, indeed, Most Honored. I do not see Thusness as the physical signs of excellence. Why do I say that? Because Thusness has taught that what is said to show the physical signs of excellence lacks the physical signs of excellence. Therefore, they are called the physical signs of excellence."

§21

"Subhuti, what do you think? Does Thusness think, 'I give a teaching'? Subhuti, do not look at it that way. A teaching that Thusness has given is not anything. Suppose, Subhuti, someone says, 'Thusness gives a teaching.' Subhuti, that person misrepresents me because he or she either does not understand or misunderstands. Why do I say that? Because, Subhuti, what is called giving a teaching is a concept. The so-called giving a teaching is not anything."

"Most Honored, in future times, will there be sentient beings who hear such presentations of the teachings and have deep faith in them?"

"Subhuti, they are not sentient beings, nor are they not sentient beings. Why do I say that? Because, Subhuti, Thusness teaches that what are called sentient beings are without sentient being. Therefore they are called 'sentient beings.'

§22

"Subhuti, what do you think? Is there any such experience as the supreme utter and complete awakening of Thusness into full and complete buddhahood?"

"Most Honored, there is no such experience as the supreme utter and complete awakening of Thusness into full and complete buddhahood."

"Subhuti, that is right, that is right. Nothing is held, not even the slightest experience. Therefore, it is called supreme full and complete awakening.

§23

"Further, Subhuti, this experience is the same as any other. It is not different in any way. That is why it is called supreme full and complete awakening. Supreme full and complete awakening is the same as any other in having no sense of self, no sentient being, no living being, and no individual being.

"Virtuous experiences bring about utter complete awakening, Subhuti. Of these so-called virtuous experiences, Thusness teaches that they are without experience at all. Therefore, they are called virtuous experiences.

§24

"Further, Subhuti, suppose a son or daughter of a noble family actually gathered and gave away mountains of the seven kinds of precious jewels, as many as there are Mount Merus in a great thousand-world-system of a billion worlds and someone memorized just a four-line verse of this perfection of wisdom and taught it to others. Subhuti, the quantity of goodness of the former would not come to a hundredth, a thousandth, or a hundred-thousandth of the latter. The latter does not permit any measure based on counting, division, tally, analogy, comparison, or genesis.

§25

"Subhuti, what do you think? Does Thusness think, 'I have freed sentient beings'? Subhuti, do not look at it that way. Why do I say that? Because, Subhuti, no sentient being is freed by Thusness. Subhuti, if Thusness freed a sentient being, right there, Thusness would have engaged a sense of self, engaged a sentient being, engaged a living being, and engaged an individual being. Subhuti, Thusness has taught that what is called engaging a sense of self has no engaging.

"However, foolish persons engage. Subhuti, Thusness has taught that these so-called foolish persons are without personhood. Therefore they are called foolish persons.

§26

"Subhuti, what do you think? Do you see Thusness by means of the physical signs of excellence?"

"No, indeed, Most Honored. I do not see Thusness by means of the physical signs of excellence."

"That is right, Subhuti. You do not see Thusness by means of the physical signs of excellence. Subhuti, if Thusness were seen by means of the physical signs of excellence, the wheel-wielding monarch would be Thusness. Therefore, do not see Thusness by means of the physical signs of excellence."

"If I understand what the Most Honored has taught, I do not see Thusness by means of the physical signs of excellence."

Then the Most Honored composed these verses for the occasion:

> Whoever sees me in form,
> Whoever knows me through sound,
> Their practice is incorrect.
> Such people do not see me.

> The Buddha is seen through true experience.
> The Guide is true presence.
> Because true experience is not an object of knowing,
> It cannot be known by ordinary consciousness.

§27

"Subhuti, what do you think? If you hold that the physical signs of excellence bring about a full and complete buddha, thusness, and saint, Subhuti, do not look at it this way. Subhuti, a full and complete buddha, thusness, and saint does not come to full buddhahood, the supreme and utter completeness of awakening, by means of the physical signs of excellence.

"Subhuti, if you hold that those who correctly enter the bodhisattva path eradicate or put an end to experience, do not look at it this way, Subhuti. All those who enter the bodhisattva path correctly do not eradicate or put an end to experience.

§28

"Further, Subhuti, compared to a son or daughter of a good family who fills as many world-systems as there are grains of sand in the Ganges valley with the seven precious jewels and gives all of them away, a bodhisattva who is able to accept that experience has no beginning and is beyond measure gives rise on that basis to a much greater quantity of goodness. Yet, Subhuti, the bodhisattva does not hold that quantity of goodness."

"Indeed, should a bodhisattva not hold that quantity of goodness, Most Honored?"

"Subhuti, although they hold it, they do not hold it incorrectly. Therefore, it is said they hold it.

§29

"Subhuti, if someone says, 'Thusness comes and goes, stands and sits, and lies down,' that person does not understand the meaning of what I explain. Why do I say that? Because, Subhuti, Thusness does not go anywhere and does not come from anywhere, and is therefore called a full and complete buddha, thusness, and saint.

§30

"Further, Subhuti, suppose a son or daughter of good family were to take as many dust particles as in a great thousand-world-system of a billion worlds and grind them into powder as fine as the finest particles, for example. Subhuti, what do you think? Would the number of finest particles in that pile be a large number?"

"Most Honored, it would, indeed. The number of finest particles in that pile would be a large number, indeed. What is the point here? The point, Most Honored, is if there were such a pile, the Most Honored would not name it a pile of the finest particles. What is the point here? The point is Thusness teaches that whatever the Most Honored says is a pile of finest particles is not a pile. Therefore, it is called a pile of the finest particles.

"Whatever Thusness teaches is a great thousand-world-system of a billion worlds, Thusness teaches that it is not a system. Therefore it is called a great thousand-world-system of a billion worlds. What is the point here? The point, Most Honored, is if there were a system, it would be held to be a solid entity. What Thusness teaches as holding to be a solid entity, Thusness teaches that that is without holding. Therefore it is called holding to be a solid entity."

"Subhuti, holding as a solid entity is a term. The experience itself is ineffable. Foolish ordinary people hold.

§31

"Subhuti, suppose someone said, 'Thusness teaches holding self. Thusness teaches holding sentient being, holding living being, and holding individual being.' Subhuti, is that the correct view?"

"Most Honored, it is not. Most Joyous, indeed, it is not. What is the point here? The point, Most Honored, is that what Thusness teaches as holding self, Thusness teaches as being without holding there. Therefore, it is called holding self."

"Subhuti, it is in this way that those who have correctly entered the bodhisattva path should know and regard all experience. Having developed faith, above all, they have the faith not to dwell even in the conceptual understanding of experience. Why do I say that? Thusness teaches that what is called the conceptual understanding of experience is without conceptual understanding. That is why it is called conceptual understanding.

§32

"Subhuti, suppose a bodhisattva-mahasattva filled innumerable, uncountable worlds with the seven precious jewels and gave them away, and suppose that a son or daughter of good family took up only a four-line verse from this The Perfection of Wisdom, cherished it, read it, took it to heart, or taught it extensively to others. On that basis, he or she would generate an incalculably, immeasurably greater amount of goodness.

"How does one teach correctly? In a way that is without teaching correctly. Therefore, it is called teaching correctly.

> A shooting star, hazy vision, or a butter lamp,
> An enchantment, a dewdrop, or a bubble,
> A dream, a flash of lightning, or a cloud,
> See the conditioned like this."

When the Most Honored had spoken, the Elder Subhuti, the monks, the bodhisattvas, the four assemblies of monks, nuns, laymen, and laywomen, and the whole world with its gods, humans, titans, and celestial choristers rejoiced and sincerely praised the Most Honored's teaching.

This completes The Noble Perfection of Wisdom known as the Vajra Cutter. Ken McLeod translated this sutra in Windsor, California, in 2025. May it light the sun of faith and inspiration in all who read it.

Acknowledgments

THIS BOOK REPRESENTS MY FIRST TRANSLATION of an actual sutra and my first translation of a text that itself is a translation from Sanskrit. I could not have put this book together without the help and support of a number of people.

Although I was aware of the *Diamond Sutra*, I had not read it until Cynthia Jurs gave me a copy of Red Pine's translation and commentary. Agnes Lin was responsible for inspiring me to read it more closely. That effort led to Peter Alan Roberts digging up a Tibetan version of the sutra for me from the massive database of the Buddhist Digital Resource Center. Still later, Paul Harrison's comments on the two interpretations of non-self planted a seed of curiosity that eventually grew into this translation.

I am especially grateful to Peter Roberts and Paul Harrison, the former for his willingness to answer my questions about the meaning and usage of certain words in Sanskrit, the latter for the meticulous scholarship in his own translation of the *Diamond Sutra*. From a comparison of my Tibetan version with Harrison's translation from the Sanskrit, it was clear that the Tibetan followed the Sanskrit very closely, and that I could rely on the Tibetan with confidence in the face of different interpretations in translations from the Chinese.

I am also grateful to Peter Roberts, Ari Goldman, and Ingrid McLeod, all of whom were always available to discuss different ways of translating key Tibetan terms.

Michael Taft and the Berkeley Alembic gave me the opportunity to teach a six-week course on the *Diamond Sutra* in July 2024. The course was invaluable as I learned from the students there why a contemporary English translation was badly needed. Further conversations with Rob Schmidt and Stuart Goodnick on their podcast *The Mystical Positivist* helped to clarify my approach.

For the translation itself, Hokai Sobol, Majda Jurich, Jim Wilson, Ann Craig, Ann Wheatley, Nick Barr, and many others provided encouragement, support, and advice on the often tricky decisions I needed to make in the English.

Finally, my thanks to Summer Russo for her help with editing the manuscript and Maureen Forys and her team at Happenstance for designing the book and helping with the publication.

Bibliography

Churinoff, George. *Vajra Cutter Sutra (The Exalted Mahayana Sutra on the Wisdom Gone Beyond called "The Vajra Cutter")*. FPMT, 2007.

Conze, Edward. *The Diamond Sutra in Sanskrit and English*. Buddhistische Gesellschaft Berlin e.V. https://www .buddhistische-gesellschaft-berlin.de/downloads /diamantsutraconze.pdf.

Griffiths, Paul J. "Buddhist Hybrid English: Some Notes on Philology and Hermeneutics for Buddhologists." *The Journal of the International Association of Buddhist Studies* 4, no. 2 (1981): 17–32.

Harrison, Paul. *Manuscripts in the Schøyen Collection. Buddhist Manuscripts Volume III*. Hermes Publishing, 2006. https:// static1.squarespace.com/static/5c03ced75ffd204418037b7a /t/5c5306ce575d1f9230da8a6a/1548945103490 /Diamond+Sutra-Paul+Harrison+tr.pdf.

Johnson, AJ. *Diamond Sutra: A New Translation of the Classic Buddhist Text*. Alex Johnson Productions, 2024. https:// diamond-sutra.com/read-the-diamond-sutra-here/.

Khenpo Sodargye. *The Diamond Cutter Sutra: A Commentary by Dzogchen Master Khenpo Sodargye*. Wisdom, 2020. Kindle.

Mu Soeng. *The Diamond Sutra: Transforming the Way We Perceive the World*. Wisdom Publications, 2000.

Muller, AC. *The Diamond Sutra.* October 26, 2013. http://
www.acmuller.net/bud-canon/diamond_sutra.html.

Red Pine. *The Diamond Sutra: Text and Commentaries Translated from Sanskrit and Chinese.* Counterpoint, 2001.

Thich Nhat Hanh. *The Diamond That Cuts through Illusion:
Commentaries on the Prajñaparamita Diamond Sutra.*
Parallax Press, 1992.

The Vajra Cutter Sutra. Tog Palace Manuscript, Tibetan
Kanjur. Vol. 51. Leh, 1979.